see your
way to
mindfulness

see your way to mindfulness

IDEAS AND INSPIRATION TO OPEN YOUR I

Written, illustrated, and photographed by

DAVID SCHILLER

WORKMAN PUBLISHING • NEW YORK

Library of Congress Cataloging-in-Publication Data is available.

ISBN 978-0-7611-8744-8

Design by Janet Vicario

Grateful acknowledgment is made for permission to reprint an excerpt of "Earth Dweller" by William Stafford from *Ask Me: 100 Essential Poems*. Copyright © 1970, 1998 by William Stafford and the Estate of William Stafford. Reprinted with the permission of The Permissions Company, Inc., on behalf of Graywolf Press, Minneapolis, Minnesota, graywolfpress.org.

Workman books are available at special discounts when purchased in bulk for premiums and sales promotions as well as for fund-raising or educational use. Special editions or book excerpts also can be created to specification. For details, contact the Special Sales Director at the address below, or send an email to specialmarkets@workman.com.

Workman Publishing Company, Inc.
225 Varick Street
New York, NY 10014-4381
workman.com

WORKMAN is a registered trademark of Workman Publishing Co., Inc.

Printed in China

First printing November 2016

10 9 8 7 6 5 4 3 2 1

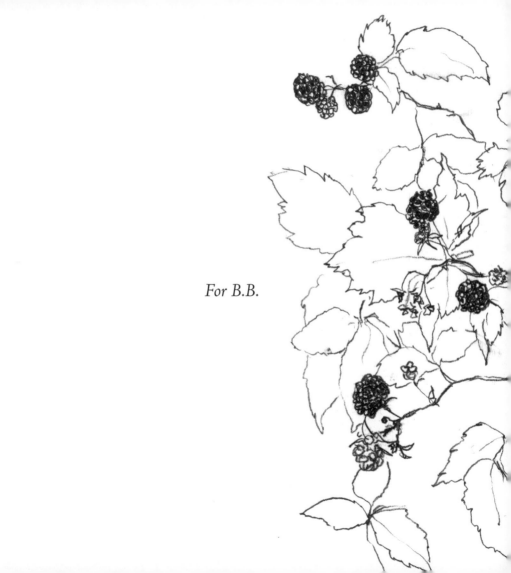

For B.B.

Introduction

In meditation, we sit and breathe and try to still our minds to experience the moment, and only the moment. Even then it's almost impossible, as a steady and random stream of thoughts clamors for our attention.

And once we're off the meditation cushion? Forget about it. It's as if society has fashioned a world whose sole purpose is to distract us from the here and now. On the one hand, our culture works relentlessly to expand its control over nature, filing down every little burr that might irritate our experience of being alive in the world. On the other, it appears we've developed a collective phobia of being un-entertained. Television, sports, movies, music, video games, the Internet, social media—we now live amid an endless rabbit hole of temptations to get lost in.

Presiding over all of it is the phone. Perhaps nothing so insidiously severs us from reality than our beautiful, responsive, indispensable smartphones. They amuse us when we're bored, guide us when we're lost, connect us when we're lonely, answer us when we're curious. All of which sounds so positive—until you sit down to dinner and notice that half the table is checking their email.

Or attend a concert, and see that large swaths of the audience are texting, tweeting, or taking pictures. Or go for a hike and discover your companion is snapchatting. Instead of experiencing the experience, we're documenting the experience. Or escaping the experience. Or sharing the experience. Anything *but* the experience. (Though this is not meant to scold. Every photo in this book, for example, was taken with an iPhone.)

Some centuries ago, a man asked the eccentric Japanese Zen teacher and poet, Ikkyū, to define the highest wisdom. Ikkyū wrote one word: *attention*. The man couldn't quite get it and asked again. Ikkyū again wrote "attention." This went on once more until the man, exasperated and annoyed, said, "What does this 'attention' mean, anyway?" "Attention means attention," Ikkyū replied.

It couldn't be simpler: The meaning of life is to pay attention, to see. Open your eyes. Reality, that which is before you, is where you live.

See Your Way to Mindfulness is about coming back to the here and now, with the presence that we call mindfulness, through the practice of intentional seeing. It is about relearning how to come face-to-face with the real—*re*learning, because it is something we knew as children. Seeing is like meditation in its directness, and like meditation it requires that we hit pause, slow down, try to let go of the endless stream of thoughts, and just focus on what's in front of us. And in the same way that meditation needs to be taught, seeing needs a little help because we're losing the ability to do it. Seeing isn't really "looking," and it's not "watching." All day we look or we watch; both activities are passive compared to active seeing. It's a little ironic, actually. As our world becomes more and more visual, we are inundated with gorgeous images to look at, and yet we are increasingly impoverished in our direct relationship with the world, especially the natural world. The immediate world of trees and flowers and long stretches of beach have so much to teach us, once we stop and take a real look.

The aim of *See Your Way to Mindfulness* is to encourage the reader to discover the joy of seeing, and through it, find a more balanced, mindful way of being. There are quotes from Buddhists and artists and philosophers extolling the importance of seeing. And there are prompts or exercises that encourage the reader to see for him- or herself. These exercises are not so much about creativity as about where creativity starts; they're about taking us back to our beginner's mind, so that we can discover the world afresh, with new eyes, and revel in the miracle of the everyday.

"The first step . . .
  shall be to lose the way."

—*Galway Kinnell*

sit still and look
until the you
disappears

Henry David Thoreau was great at sitting still. He could be a spectator watching an ant war for eight hours straight, or sit all morning on his front step at Walden Pond, watching the sun climb overhead. Hunters and fishermen do this, too. They find a spot in the woods or a stream and hold still for so long that they blend into the natural surroundings. This also has the effect of sharpening their powers of observation. Try it yourself, in the woods or at a park or, like Thoreau, at a pond. There's always some kind of wildlife around, birds or squirrels or frogs. Sit until you become part of the silence. Chances are a bird won't land on your shoulder, but a butterfly might. Then see—or hear—what the world is like without you in it.

→

Just sit and watch the river flow, and the world will slowly reveal itself.

"In all things of nature there is something of the marvelous."

—*Aristotle*

"This is your world; it is your feast. . . . Look at the greatness of the whole thing. Look! Don't hesitate—look! Open your eyes. Don't blink, and look, look—look further."

—*Chögyam Trungpa*

" **I** am doing something I learned early to do, I am paying attention to small beauties, whatever I have—as if it were our duty to find things to love, to bind ourselves to this world."

—*Sharon Olds*

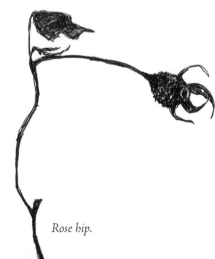

Rose hip.

look for what is changing
(p.s. everything changes)

We're all told to live in the moment. And yet we all walk down the street or drive along the road, and it all looks the same as it did yesterday and will tomorrow, and we scarcely pay attention. So what is this magical "moment"? Well, try to imagine what won't be the same tomorrow. That certain slant of light. The mood you're in *right now* because of a dream you had. The way a light breeze is chasing away the morning humidity. That's the moment. To paraphrase the Greek philosopher Heraclitus, you can never step in the same river twice. Does it matter? That's like asking, *Does life matter?*

→

Some things change right before our eyes, others change over years. Or centuries.

"The moment one gives close attention to anything, even a blade of grass, it becomes a mysterious, awesome, indescribably magnificent world in itself."

—*Henry Miller*

"Don't think, look!"

—Ludwig Wittgenstein

Two branches of rhododendron.

"More wisdom is latent in things as they are than in all the words men use."

—*Antoine de Saint-Exupéry*

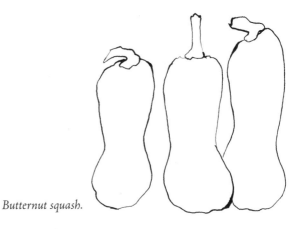

Butternut squash.

look up

Stand under a tree and look up! In all seasons, this affords an endlessly interesting moment. When leaves are on the trees, the play of light, shadow, and color—particularly in the fall—is dazzling. Start taking photographs. The images will have the uncentered energy of an oriental rug. A different kind of reward awaits you in winter. It takes greater effort, but as you look more and more attentively, the unique structure of each tree, like its skeleton, reveals itself. As do unfallen fruit, the last stubborn leaves, and abandoned nests, belonging to wasps, squirrels, and birds.

→

See the passage of time in a new way, and take comfort in the cycle of seasons.

"The true mystery of the world is the visible, not the invisible."

—*Oscar Wilde*

"One can travel the world and see nothing. To achieve understanding it is necessary not to see many things, but to look hard at what you do see."

—*Giorgio Morandi*

"The eye awakened is the eye in love."

—*Frederick Franck*

Clump of downy lamb's ears.

appreciate the imperfect

Perfection is, well, boring. As Edgar Allan Poe said, "There is no exquisite beauty . . . without some strangeness in the proportion." And as it relates to the presentation of natural things—flowers, a piece of fruit, the human face—perfect beauty is a specious goal, preying on our innate preference for symmetry and pleasingness to cover up a lack of authenticity. Think about the supermarket tomato. Sure, it looks pretty—but it's also pretty tasteless. It's eye candy. Next time you visit a local farmers' market, try to shop in a way that's counter to those aesthetic prejudices. Then start looking at other things that challenge the idea of perfection, and discover the innate beauty of the imperfect. In Japan, this quality is called *wabi-sabi*.

→

Spoiler alert: The world is filled with things that challenge our desire for perfection. Relish them.

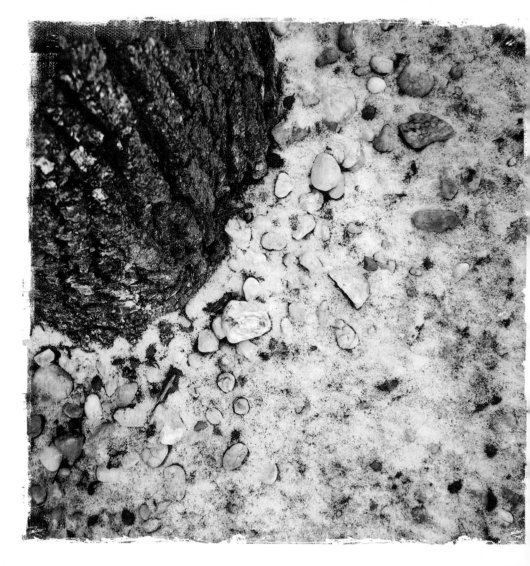

"**Y**ou need to let the little things that would ordinarily bore you suddenly thrill you."

—*Andy Warhol*

"Ralph Waldo Emerson once asked what we would do if the stars only came out once every thousand years. No one would sleep that night, of course. The world would become religious overnight. We would be ecstatic, delirious, made rapturous by the glory of God. Instead the stars come out every night, and we watch television."

—*Paul Hawken*

draw what you see

Blind contour drawing is a classic beginner's exercise that leads to surprising results. The setup is simple: Sit at a table with your pencil hovering over a large blank sheet of paper. Hold the pencil in one hand and curl your other hand into a fist or another interesting shape. Study the shape and begin, very slowly, to draw what you see. This should take at least 20 minutes. Look at every millimeter of your hand, but don't look at your sketch. When your eye follows a complex wrinkle, for example, the pencil should be recording it like the stylus on an EKG or lie detector. Follow the curve of every knuckle, the line of every wrinkle. Only when you feel you've examined every part of your hand should you look at your drawing. Its little squiggles and lines will be full of life.

→

Follow the curves of the leaf, the arc of the stem, the soft contour of the petal. You'll see something you hadn't before.

"Now I know why people worship, carry around magic emblems, wake up talking dreams they teach to their children: the world speaks. The world speaks everything to us. It is our only friend."

—*William Stafford*

"The more you draw, the more you see and then you start seeing everywhere..."

—David Hockney

Four purple figs.

"Putting the whole of your mind/body into the act of seeing . . ."

—*Dōgen*

Bittersweet vine.

take a
closer look

Seeds in the flesh of a strawberry. The veins of a leaf. A fly, rubbing its antennae together. Bark on a tree, snowflakes on a car window. Pick up a handful of sand and study its thousands of glittering bits. Can you see the world in those grains of sand?

→

Zoom in. The bark and pruned limbs become a yin-yang, the carpet of gingko leaves a work of art.

"How can the divine Oneness be seen? In beautiful forms, breathtaking wonders, awe-inspiring miracles?

The Tao is not obliged to present itself in this way.

If you are willing to be lived by it, you will see it everywhere, even in the most ordinary things."

—Lao-tzu

"Isn't it enough to see that a garden is beautiful without having to believe that there are fairies at the bottom of it too?"

—*Douglas Adams*

spend 30 minutes taking a 5-minute walk

This one can be challenging, especially for anyone who lives in a city. The pace of life on the sidewalks is fast. It feels good. We're often driven that way internally, too. Some of us even want our walks to count as training. Which is why "slow down" is a ubiquitous counter-mantra. But how slow? How about as slow as can be. Think of it as walking meditation, what Zen Buddhists call *kinhin*. Take a step, breathe, look. Study the bark on a tree. Examine something in a store window. Allow yourself to be completely distracted from the goal of reaching your destination. You'll fight it, but if and when you're able to let go of the tug to "hurry up," you might just discover a new experience.

→

Look far, look close—what will you see with the luxury of time?

"As soon as you see something, you already start to intellectualize it. As soon as you intellectualize something, it is no longer what you saw."

—*Shunryu Suzuki*

"What is the meaning of life? That was all—a simple question; one that tended to close in on one with years. The great revelation had never come. The great revelation perhaps never did come. Instead there were little daily miracles, illuminations, matches struck unexpectedly in the dark . . ."

—*Virginia Woolf*

Skeleton of grilled sardine.

"If the sight of the blue skies fills you with joy, if a blade of grass springing up in the fields has power to move you, if the simple things of nature have a message that you understand, rejoice, for your soul is alive."

—*Eleonora Duse*

Dried clethra.

carry a journal

If you're a writer, you're probably already doing this. If not, try it out. Pack a pocket-size journal and take it with you everywhere. Look, and then record. If it doesn't come naturally, start with something simple, such as the date and the weather. Or pick a time, like 2:15 p.m., and keep that as a daily appointment to write down one thing you see.

→

What turns up? What never goes away? Does deliberately noticing these changes—or lack thereof—change your perception?

"**B**lessed are they who see beautiful things in humble places where other people see nothing."

—*Camille Pissarro*

"The foolish reject what they see, not what they think; the wise reject what they think, not what they see."

—*Huang Po*

"The point of Buddhism is to *just see.*
That's all."

—*Steve Hagen*

Rose of Sharon.

see beyond
the name

Names are brilliant shortcuts to efficient communication, but they often prevent us from seeing the individual identity of an object. When we hear the sentence "She climbed a tree," most of us will begin by imagining a generic tree, like a dictionary photo. Here's an interesting—or perhaps maddening—exercise to sharpen your verbal powers of seeing: Have a conversation with someone without ever using the names for things. How would you say "Hand me that pencil?" or "I think it's time you mowed the lawn." You'd have to come up with creative descriptors, and perhaps your conversation partner will have a different understanding of a particular object's purpose (that's the maddening part). Either way, it leads to a richer version of describing what you see.

→

By calling it a rose, it may prevent you from seeing further. What happens when you call it "a flower with thorns"?

"When you no longer make any distinction between the water of this pool and the water of the Ganges, then you will know that you have Perfect Knowledge."

—*Ramakrishna*

"The world is holy. We are holy. All life is holy. Daily prayers are delivered on the lips of breaking waves, the whisperings of grasses, the shimmering of leaves."

—*Terry Tempest Williams*

Asiatic day flower.

"Life is misery, and miraculous beauty. The word 'miracle' has been used too often and has lost its value. But we live in miracles. The thrushes in the park, the ducks drifting on the canals, the floating seagulls, but also the car on the highway, the mechanical digger in the polder and the large square apartment blocks. Whoever can take the time and the peace to observe is surprised and feels the void of his own being."

—*Janwillem van de Wetering*

see the world like a picture

Windows, in a window frame, frame. The function of a window is to bring in light. The pleasure of a window is to let us look out into the world. Like most pleasures, it means most when it's contained. A window limits the field where our eyes might roam, enhancing, by this concentration—this *framing*—the joy we take in seeing. Emily Dickinson, who spent much of her reclusive life looking at the outside world through the many windows in her home in Amherst, Massachusetts, linked windows with the power and possibilities of poetry. Windows are not prose.

Next time you pass a window, linger. Sit. Seek out your favorite window, or join the writers and daydreamers and perch in the window of a local café. Then use the window like a meditation cushion. The frame is a tool to help us turn what we see into a picture, the way the cushion supports our body and makes it easy for us to sit. And then we're ready to get up—to get off the cushion, to eliminate the frame, to see on our own.

→

Look through a window as a frame. Does what you see now look like a painting?

"Why, who makes much of a miracle?
  As to me I know nothing else but miracles . . .

  To me every hour of the light and dark is a miracle,
  Every cubic inch of space is a miracle."

—*Walt Whitman*

find the mushroom

Mushroom hunters talk about this all the time, especially when it comes to morels: You can be looking right at a perfectly good specimen and simply not see it. And then it pops into view, as if it just appeared at that moment! Of course it didn't— you were just ready to see it. After that the hunt is on, because once you spot the first mushroom, you begin to see others. Your eyes are ready; your mind is open. Try it next time you're in a woodsy area: Look for a mushroom. Then, see if finding more becomes easier. In a sense, this exercise is not about finding one mushroom, but three, or five, or a dozen. In the city, try the same thing with coins or register receipts. The probability of a lot of coins turning up on the street is not as great as for a patch of mushrooms in the woods, but you will begin to see all sorts of wonderful things you never expected.

→

When you find a mushroom, it's like a switch goes on. Suddenly you can't stop searching for them.

"I never saw an ugly thing in my life."

—*John Constable*

let the shadow
tell its story

What a funny thing a shadow is. It is not quite real, yet it is wholly natural. The shadow of a tree is less like the real tree casting the shadow than a drawing or photograph, not only because the shadow conveys just a part of the tree, in its flatness, but also because it's "interpreted," though in this case not by the eye of the artist but the angle of the sun (or moon, if you're lucky, particularly on newly fallen snow). Spend some time looking at shadows; they're everywhere in the daytime. Stripped of color, detail, and mass, the shadow reveals an elemental essence of the thing being seen.

It's suddenly fresh.

→

When we pay attention to the shadow of something, we see it for what it is—but in a new way.

"If only we could pull out our brain and use only our eyes."

—*Pablo Picasso*

"The world is full of magic things,
patiently waiting for our senses to
grow sharper."

—W. B. Yeats

here's looking at you

A dozen, a hundred, a thousand selfies later, do you really know what you look like? Rembrandt, Van Gogh, and Picasso created the original selfies in searching and painfully honest self-portraits. So did Zen masters like Hakuin, capturing the great intensity of a teacher in his bold inky brush. Put aside for a moment what your face expresses about your personality. Can you describe the shape of your eyes, the width of your nostrils, the height of your forehead or arc of your mouth? You've seen your face your whole life. Now, really look at it. Not at a photo, but sitting for a good long time in front of a mirror. When the self-consciousness comes, try not to let it get the better of you. This is not about vanity. It's an act of exploration—of real seeing.

→

Focus on a single body part; linger in the three-way mirror. Take a selfie on the beach. Wait! Who is that?

"It is looking at things for a long time that ripens you and gives you a deeper understanding."

—*Vincent van Gogh*

"There is a road from the eye to the heart that does not go through the intellect."

—G. K. Chesterton

"The only thing is *to see*."

—*Auguste Rodin*

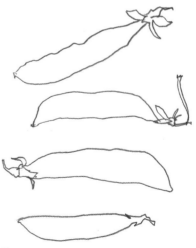

Sugar snap peas.

shoot first, look later

When we bring the camera up to our eye or hold our smartphone in that ubiquitous picture-taking position, we're making an aesthetic decision of what we think is the best way to "see" the scene or object that's piqued our interest. For many of us, the camera becomes our second, more focused eye, an extension of our whole being. But imagine unlinking your eye and your camera. Actually, imagine unlinking your *brain* and your camera. Next time you're out, take your camera along and skip the pointing—just shoot. Hold it at arm's length, close your eyes, turn, and shoot. Do it again and again. Your camera becomes a pure eye, tethered only by the range of your arm, looking at things or places that you would never bother to notice. Later, go through the pictures. What did it "see"? What did you miss?

→

Let your camera show you beauty you might have overlooked, and soon you'll start seeing it on your own.

"Value judgments are destructive to our proper business, which is curiosity and awareness."

—*John Cage*

look up, way up

Remember finding figures and faces in clouds? Or searching for shooting stars? Try it with fresh eyes. First, find the right spot: soft grass beneath an open sky. In the daytime, watch the clouds. You can start by looking for familiar shapes—that in itself is an act of paying attention. But can you take it one step further, relishing the clouds as clouds, simply enjoying them for their fluffy loveliness?

Then, in the nighttime, turn your attention to a different phenomenon. The best way to look for shooting stars is not to stare at any one spot, but rather to keep your focus open, neutral, lightly scanning. Think of your eyes as a wide-angle lens. You may begin to get lost as the starlight comes in and out of focus, bringing with it thoughts about eternity and infinity. But if you're lucky, a shooting star will snap you back to attention—a real glimpse of the miraculous.

→

How does our world change when we look as far as the eye can see? Then imagine the moon or birds looking back. How does it feel to be the speck?

"Choose only one master—Nature."

—*Rembrandt van Rijn*

"It is not meaning that we need but sight."

—*Lawrence Durrell*

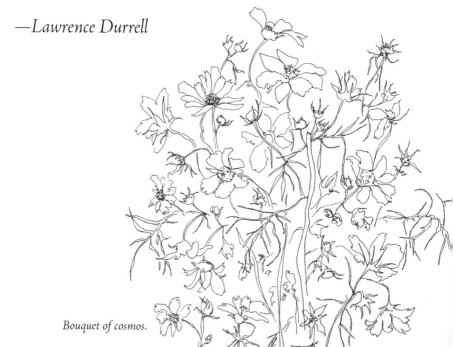

Bouquet of cosmos.

"If we knew that tonight we were going to go blind, we would take a longing, last real look at every blade of grass, every cloud formation, every speck of dust, every rainbow, raindrop—everything."

—*Pema Chödrön*

see without judgment

Is there a more judgmental word than "beautiful"? Layers and layers of habit, evolution, training, memory, and more cause our eyes to snap into focus at the sight of something conventionally beautiful, be it a face or a flower. It's like we're trapped into valuing only what's pretty. Hence, for example, the shock of modern art. Is Pollock beautiful? Yes, if you retrain your eyes—or see without judgment. Try it. Find the ugly or the ordinary interesting enough to really look at. And discover a truth—that without judgment, everything is beautiful.

→

Keep those flowers past their "prime," and discover new riches—just because something fades (like us!) doesn't make it less beautiful.

"To see is to forget the name of the thing one sees."

—*Paul Valéry*

draw
in motion

If you like to draw, try this exercise inspired by the British artist David Hockney via the ancient Chinese art of painting on a scroll instead of a fixed canvas. All you need is a pen or pencil and a Moleskine Japanese album—a special sketchbook with one continuous sheet of blank paper folded into 60 accordion pages. The plan is to go for a long walk and every few minutes stop, look, sketch something that catches your eye, and repeat. No need to fill the entire notebook the first time out, and no need to stress over the quality of the drawings. Just capture your walk. Later, spread out the pages—you've opened up your own time line of seeing.

→

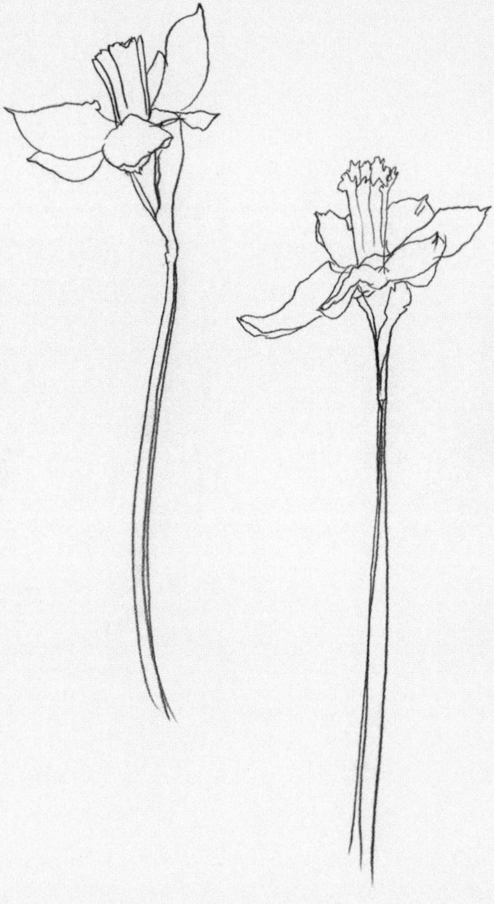

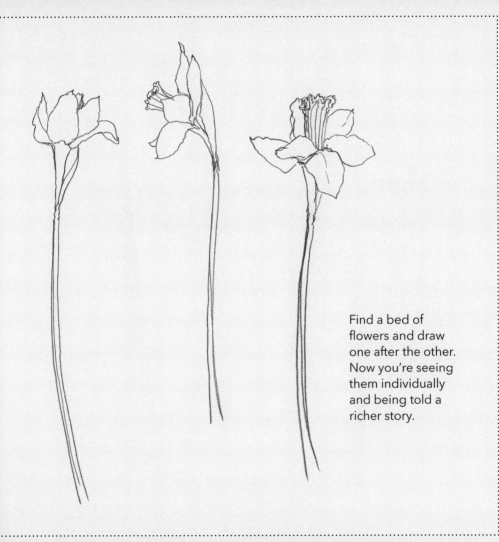

Find a bed of flowers and draw one after the other. Now you're seeing them individually and being told a richer story.

"The most beautiful thing in the world is, of course, the world itself."

—*Wallace Stevens*

"Nobody sees a flower—really—it is so small it takes time—we haven't time—and to see takes time, like to have a friend takes time."

—Georgia O'Keeffe

Echinacea, aka Coneflower.

"The ordinary, could we but see it,
   is just as extraordinary as the highest
consciousness imaginable."

—*Robert Irwin*

look down!

People, alone among the animals, walk upright on two legs in order to see the sky. What are we missing that all the other creatures see with their eyes looking down? The ground is like the floor, something we walk on but don't pay much attention to. In fact, kids growing up in the city will sometimes call the ground in the woods the "floor," a disconcerting metaphor. But look at how rich it is! Roots curl and twist. Tiny plants like snowdrops spring up while the ground's still frozen. Leaves look like Matisse cutouts. Even the city sidewalk reveals beautiful patterns and textures.

Change your point of view and discover that the streets are paved with gold.

"Whoever you are, go out into the evening, leaving your room, of which you know every bit; your house is the last before the infinite, whoever you are."

—*Rainer Maria Rilke*

"Soon the child's clear eye is clouded over by ideas and opinions, preconceptions and abstractions. Simple free being becomes encrusted with the burdensome armor of the ego. Not until years later does an instinct come that a vital sense of mystery has been withdrawn. The sun glints through the pines, and the heart is pierced in a moment of beauty and strange pain, like a memory of paradise. After that day . . . we become seekers."

—*Peter Matthiessen*

see the light

The pale light and muted colors of dawn. Dappled sunlight in a forest glade. The pinky-blue light of sunset, leading to dusk, what the French call *l'heure bleu* (you know exactly what that feels like if you've ever walked along a country road at the very end of the day). There is light that makes nothing look good—an overhead fluorescent lamp. And light that makes everything look good—a warm flickering candle. More than any other visual ingredient—color, shape, pattern, and so on—light influences how we feel about what we see. Come back to a favorite spot on different kinds of days, in different weather. How does the light change how you see? Wake up to watch the sky gradually lighten, take that walk in the country at dusk, make a date with the full moon. We live in different light all the time, but are inured to it. Light is so pervasive it's easily ignored, and attending to the quality of light will bring you more into the moment of what you're seeing. But there's something more, too—pleasure! Next time you're having dinner, light a few candles. It changes everything.

→

Light is the ultimate storyteller, but can you see just the light and not the story?

"**D**o not search. That which is, is.
Stop and see."

—*Osho*

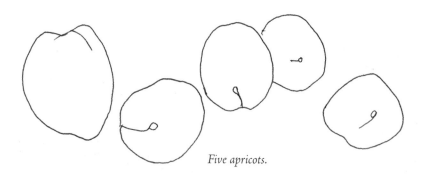

Five apricots.

"How beautiful the world was when one looked at it without searching . . . just looked, simply and innocently."

—*Hermann Hesse*

"And then there is the world of little things, seen all too seldom. Many children, perhaps because they themselves are small and closer to the ground than we, notice and delight in the small and inconspicuous . . . it is easy to share with them the beauties we usually miss because we look too hastily, seeing the whole and not its parts."

—*Rachel Carson*

eye spy
with my
open i

Children don't need to be taught how to see. Up to a certain age, the world is endlessly interesting. Recapture that magical feeling by playing I Spy, the classic guessing game, with a friend—or better yet, a child—to inject a bit of silly fun into the challenge of really looking.

→

An abandoned bird's egg, a broken stem—the great part of playing this game with kids is that they show us what's worth our attention.

"The artist has to look at everything as though he saw it for the first time; he has to look at life as he did when he was a child. . . . The first step toward creation is to see everything as it really is, and that demands a constant effort."

—*Henri Matisse*

nothing to see

Artists call the blank areas around an object *negative space*. Spread your hand and hold it up to the sky. The area between your fingers and around the outside of your arm is the negative space. Negative space is a shape with no name. It's a nothing. But it's a nothing that's everywhere. When you start seeing negative space, it opens a different window onto the world. It's not easy to do, because our eye always goes for the positive—we see the doughnut, not the hole. But what would a doughnut be without the hole?

→

Is it branches with sky, or sky with branches?

Road with stripe, or stripe with road?

"Everything that is made beautiful and fair and lovely is made for the eye of one who sees."

—*Rumi*

"The greatest thing a human soul ever does in this world is to *see* something, and tell what it *saw* in a plain way. . . . To see clearly is poetry, prophecy, and religion— all in one."

—*John Ruskin*

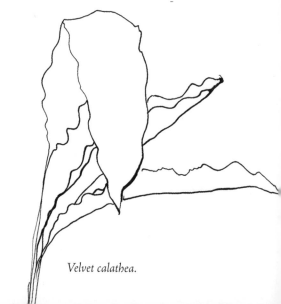

Velvet calathea.

"Stare. It is the way to educate your eye, and more. Stare, pry, listen, eavesdrop. Die knowing something. You are not here long."

—*Walker Evans*

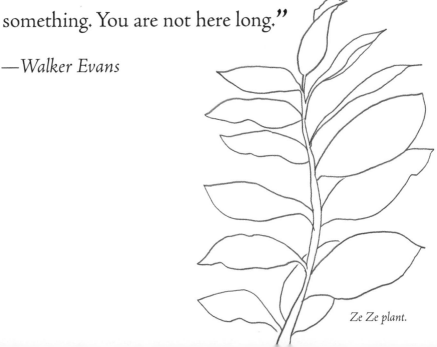

Ze Ze plant.

find new words to describe what you see

Unless you're a poet, you tend to hurry through language like everything else in life, grabbing at easy words and familiar phrases. To call an apple "red" gets the job done, but at the expense of the identity of that specific apple. Try this: Spend the time to look, really look, at that apple—or flower, or tree, or cat, or seashell—and find seven words to describe it, based on what you're seeing at that moment. After three or four, it gets hard. Try to push through. What do you discover about language, vision, and ideas?

→

Round. Husk. Pale green . . . Long, pink, shells, multiples . . . What comes after the easy words?

"The little things in life are as interesting as the big ones."

—Henry David Thoreau

see what's happening in the rain

"If the doors of perception were cleansed . . ." begins a line from the poet William Blake's "The Marriage of Heaven and Hell." A century and a half later, Aldous Huxley cleansed his "doors of perception" with mescaline. But a little rain works, too. Next time the weather turns, put on your boots and take a walk, with or without a camera. Notice how the combination of reflective water and the moist, ambiently lit gray sky brings out a fresh depth of color and richness of detail in what you see. Or notice the way the rain itself acts like a filter, creating a scene like an impressionist painting. A bright, sunny day is a lovely thing, but as every photographer knows, the light washes out the objects it hits. Rain, on the other hand, enhances and transforms.

→

From painterly beauty to hyper-reality, rain changes how we see.

"The invariable mark of wisdom is to see the miraculous in the common."

—*Ralph Waldo Emerson*

look for
the overlooked

Poets see the world as clearly as artists or scientists do. And poets also relay images to a reader. In fact, at the beginning of the 20th century, there was a movement called Imagism, which drew its inspiration from Ezra Pound's directive, "direct treatment of the thing." In other words, just present the core image, without philosophizing or unnecessary embellishment. No poem conveys this as universally as William Carlos Williams's "The Red Wheelbarrow." Or as tantalizingly. Williams challenges us with the first stanza: "So much depends / upon". What does so much depend upon? How we *see* that red wheelbarrow. Next time you're out looking, pick a humble object at random—a downed branch, a crushed cup in the gutter—and think about what depends upon it. Mimic the poem if you're inspired, but mostly try to think about the central thought: Why does so much depend upon this item?

→

If you believe, as Buddhists do, that everything is connected, then everything really does depend on a goldenrod gall or an acorn. (If you don't believe it, looking closer might convince you.)

"The real miracle is not to walk either on water or thin air but to walk on earth!"

—*Thich Nhat Hanh*

"Each moment is absolute, alive, and significant. The frog leaps, the cricket sings, a dewdrop glitters on the lotus leaf, a breeze passes through the pine branches and the moonlight falls on the murmuring stream."

—*D. T. Suzuki*

Dried branch of echinacea.

"In order to see birds, it is necessary
to become part of the silence."

—*Robert Lind*

Solomon's seal.

pick a single spot and look again and again

In his quietly brilliant book, *The Forest Unseen*, the author David George Haskell, a professor of biology, describes how he brings his students into the woods, each with a Hula-Hoop. One by one the students drop their hoops on the forest floor, and that circle marks the boundary of the world they will study for the semester. What tiny piece of the world could you come back to again and again? A corner of the yard? The edge of a pond or inlet of a local stream? An off-the-beaten-path spot in the woods? Describe what you see, then come back a week later. Now what do you see?

→

One day you'll return to the pond's edge and discover the wild iris in bloom, or see beetles hatched and munching on a fungus that wasn't there yesterday. What will be there tomorrow?

"The day is coming when a single carrot, freshly observed, will set off a revolution."

—*Paul Cézanne*

follow a stranger

It's impossible to encounter the world in a genuinely random way, at least without outside help. That's a great part of the magic of travel: The disorientation of a foreign place excites our senses, and our eyes drink in everything. But imagine that you want to encounter your backyard afresh—say, Central Park for a longtime New Yorker. Instead of trying to simulate randomness, which is almost impossible, let someone else lead the way. Follow a stranger! Now you're heading off in a direction based on . . . who knows what? It's out of your hands. Also, because it's a slightly transgressive act, your eyes will be on high alert.

$\rightarrow$

It's like déjà vu in reverse—you know you've been here before, and yet it all feels new.

"The summer moon hung full in the sky. For the time being, it was the great fact in the world."

—*Willa Cather*

Daylilies.

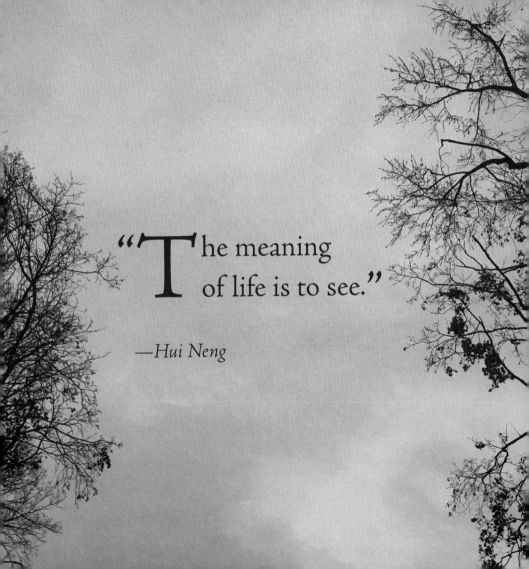

"The meaning of life is to see."

—Hui Neng

a short and arbitrary reading list

THE ZEN OF SEEING, Frederick Franck • The Dutch artist, writer, humanitarian, and lifelong Zen enthusiast left behind a beautiful body of work, including this masterpiece which argues that the activity he calls "seeing/drawing" *is* meditation.

DRAWING ON THE RIGHT SIDE OF THE BRAIN, Betty Edwards • Insight into the process of drawing, which is really about seeing—and that rarest of books that can actually teach the reader a new skill.

BUDDHISM, PLAIN AND SIMPLE, Steve Hagen • A brilliantly simple and accessible introduction to Buddhism and its deep connection to awareness.

SEEING IS FORGETTING THE NAME OF THE THING ONE SEES, Lawrence Weschler • Fascinating conversations with Robert Irwin, an artist whose career is about perception. Irwin is also quite the character—a genuine original. Pair it with Lawrence Weschler's companion book on David Hockney, TRUE TO LIFE.

SHAMBHALA: THE SACRED PATH OF THE WARRIOR, Chögyam Trungpa • We should all aspire to be a "warrior," which includes training to see the world directly in front of you.

ZEN MIND, BEGINNER'S MIND, Shunryu Suzuki • A classic that cannot be recommended enough. Suzuki taught that our true purpose "is to see things as they are."

Acknowledgments

A special thank-you to Janet Vicario for the beautiful design and visual partnership; to Mary Ellen O'Neill for her helpful suggestions and continued enthusiasm; and to Suzie Bolotin for being so supportive.

You May Also Like

The Little Zen Companion
by David Schiller

While seeking neither to define Zen nor to answer its riddles, this compilation brings together sayings, parables, haiku, koan, poetry, and other words from both Eastern and Western sources. Its maverick spirit points to a different way of looking at the world: directly, openly, joyously.

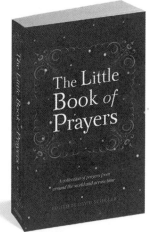

The Little Book of Prayers
Edited by David Schiller

Gathered from poets and theologians, spirituals, private letters, and holy books, this collection of common and uncommon prayers is a celebration of timeless words that allows our deepest self to shine through.